My Little Self

Losing Ego and Finding Oneness

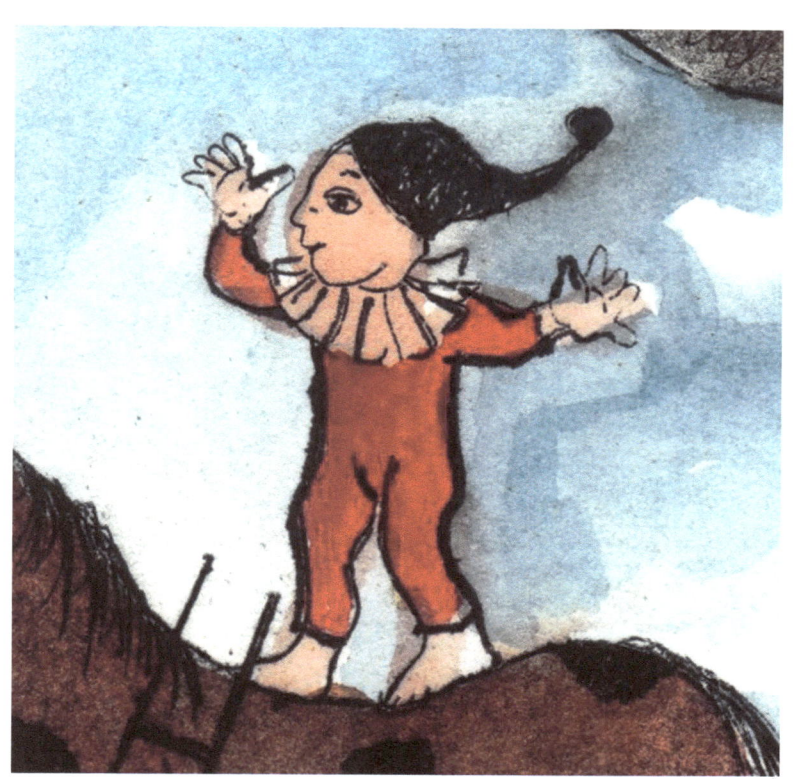

By
Ann Otis

My Little Self

© 2010 by Ann Otis

Printed in the United States of America

TO LLEWELLYN VAUGHN-LEE

Like
the ground
turning green
in a spring wind.
Like birdsong
beginning inside the egg.
Like this universe
coming into existence,
the lover wakes and whirls
in a dancing joy
then kneels down in praise.

Rumi

ACKNOWLEDGEMENTS

I gratefully thank my two beloved teachers: Llewellyn Vaughn-Lee, a Sufi Sheik, and David Driesbach, a printmaker and retired professor from Northern Illinois University. My skill in etching was fostered by David Driesbach; my skill in listening to my heart came from sitting with Llewellyn Vaughn-Lee.

Thank you to my partner, Bill; my friend and editor, Hilda Brown; my book designer, Heinz Kagerer, and my family and friends. All of you have walked along the path with me. I am blessed.

Ann Otis
New River, October 2007

PREFACE

In searching for my True Self, First I had to meet and conquer My Little Self. This lifetime journey of discovery became a reality and a necessity when, asking for guidance, images pervaded my dreams, my meditations, and my consciousness.

Over four years as these depictions of my journey appeared, I transferred them to copper plates, bit them, inked them, and then printed the plates. One by one, and not necessarily in order, the images made their way into my awareness. Not until I saw the completed pictures in full color did I understand the metamorphosis my creative soul was undergoing.

This experience of letting go to my Higher Self, and trusting my inner guidance, led me down the path I had chosen as an artist and an evolving human. It opened my heart and my consciousness to new adventures.

My journey continues as I expand my vision including making these images available so that others will be inspired to follow their own path to truth.

INFLATION

"How insignificant I am. I need to inflate myself so I can be seen. That's more like it. Now I stand out in the crowd!"

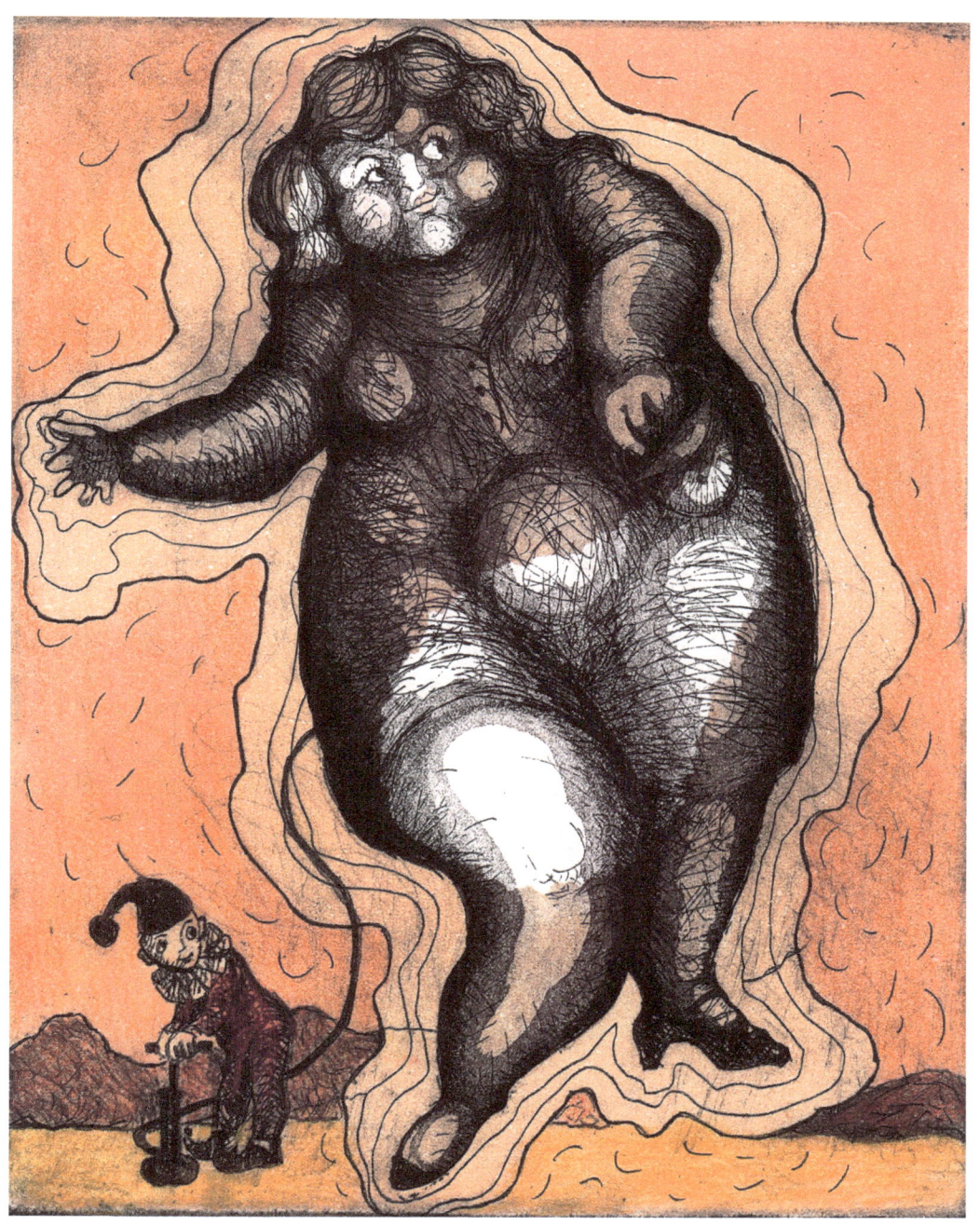

SSSSST!

"All the hot air is going out of me.
The Source has pricked my
ballooning ego."

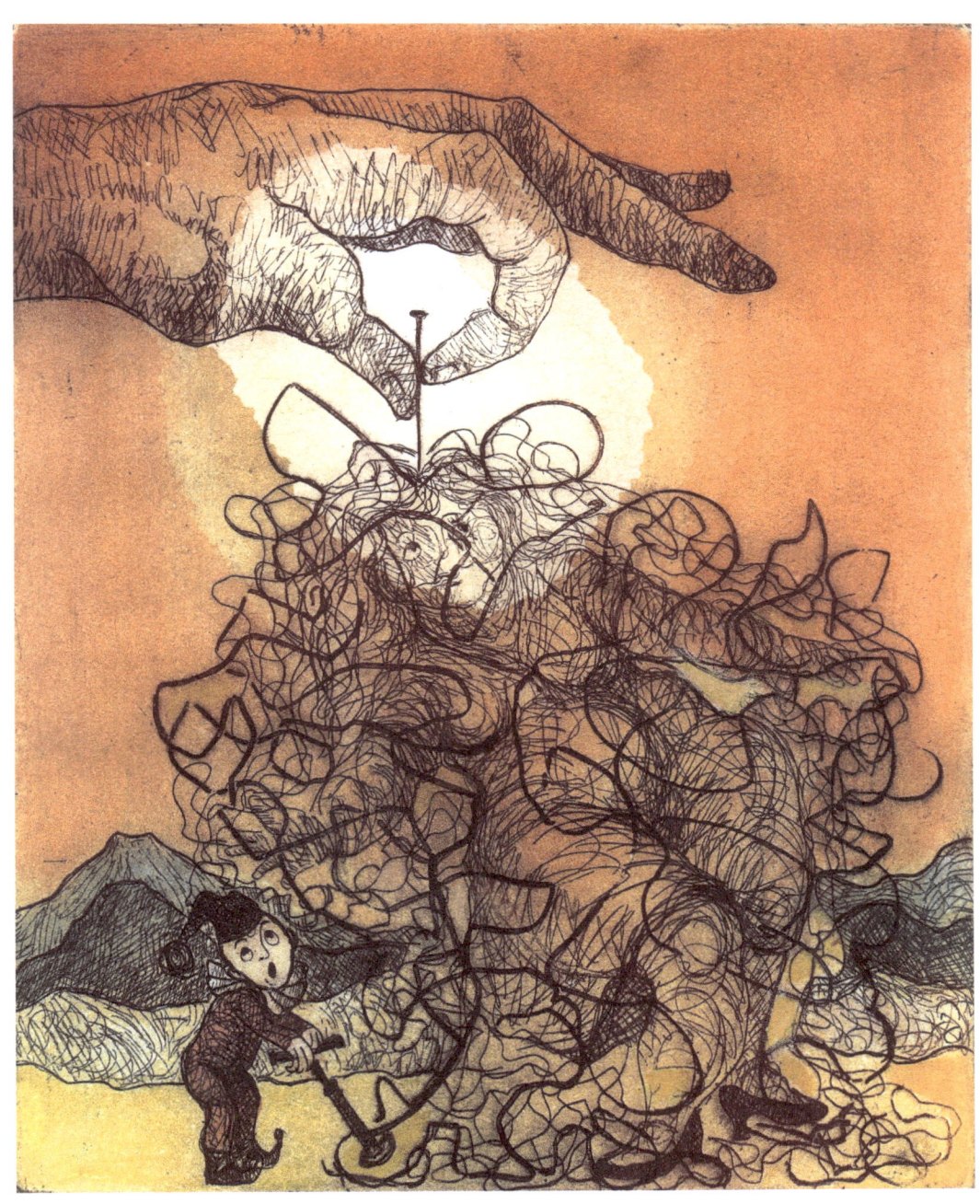

NAKED

"I'm naked and deflated. Woe is
me. Turn around don't look at me!"

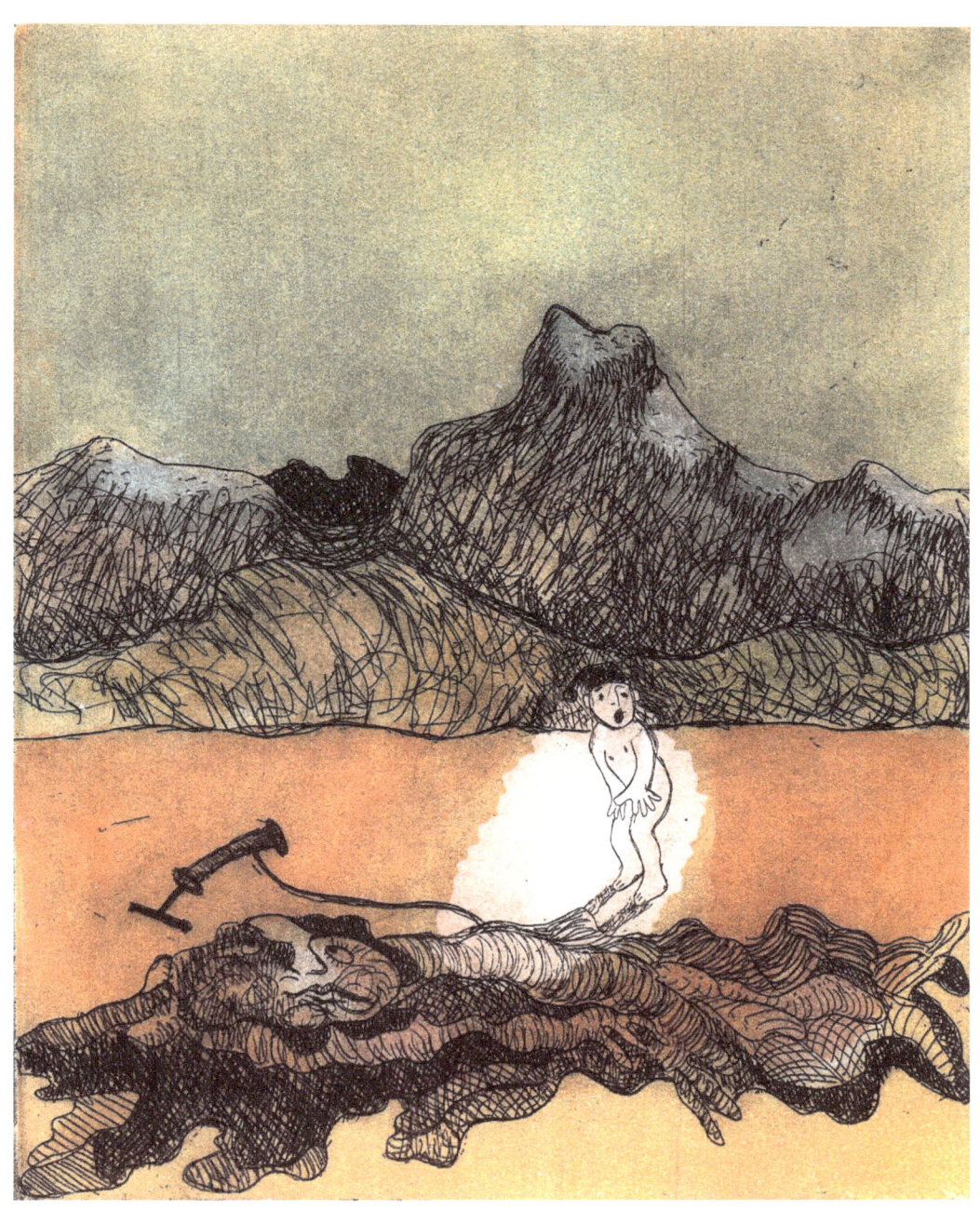

A HELPING HAND

The Source offers a helping hand. "I can do it alone. I don't need you," I jeer.

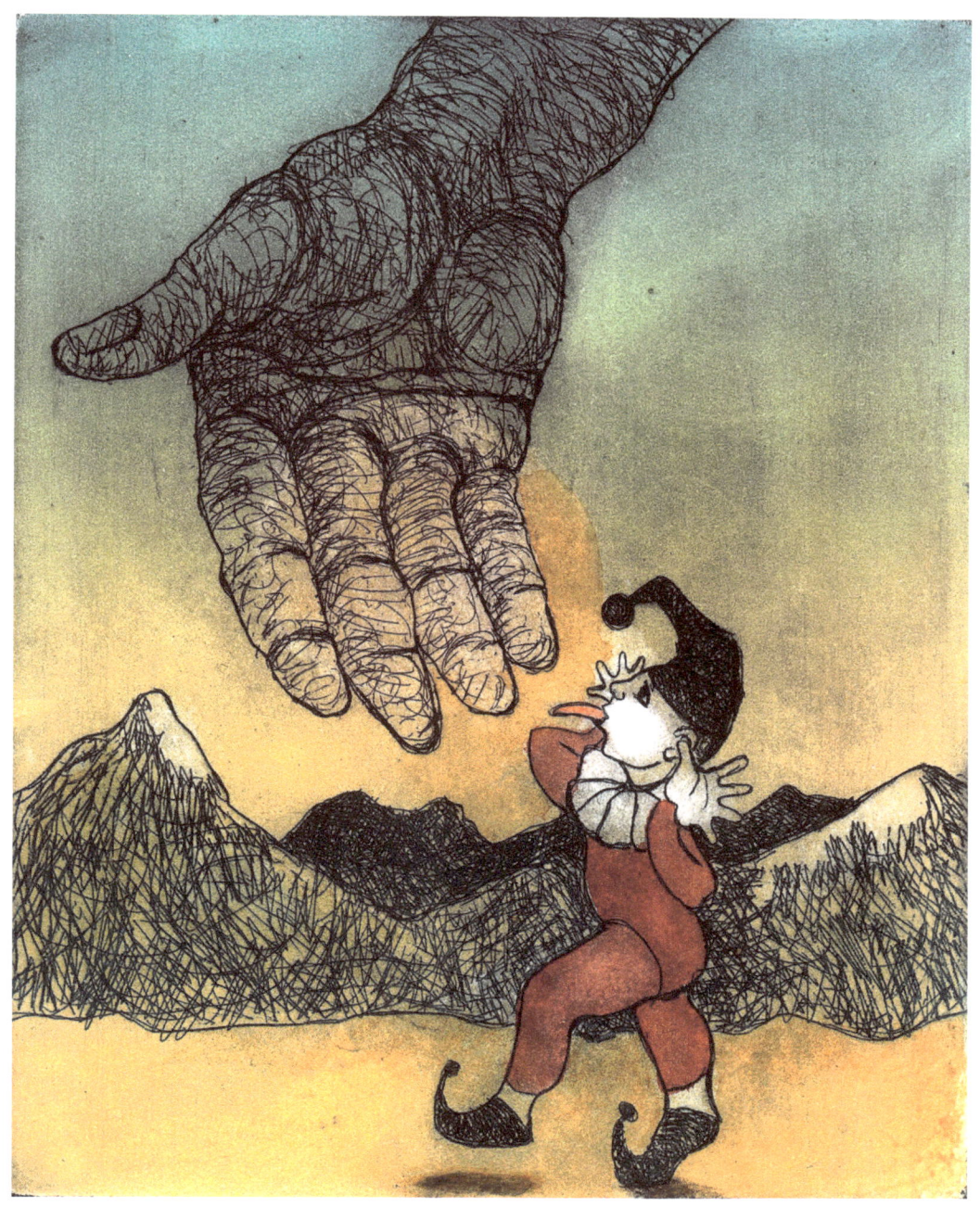

I AM BRAINY!

"I am smart. I am logical. I have a high I.Q. I am self sufficient. I know it all."

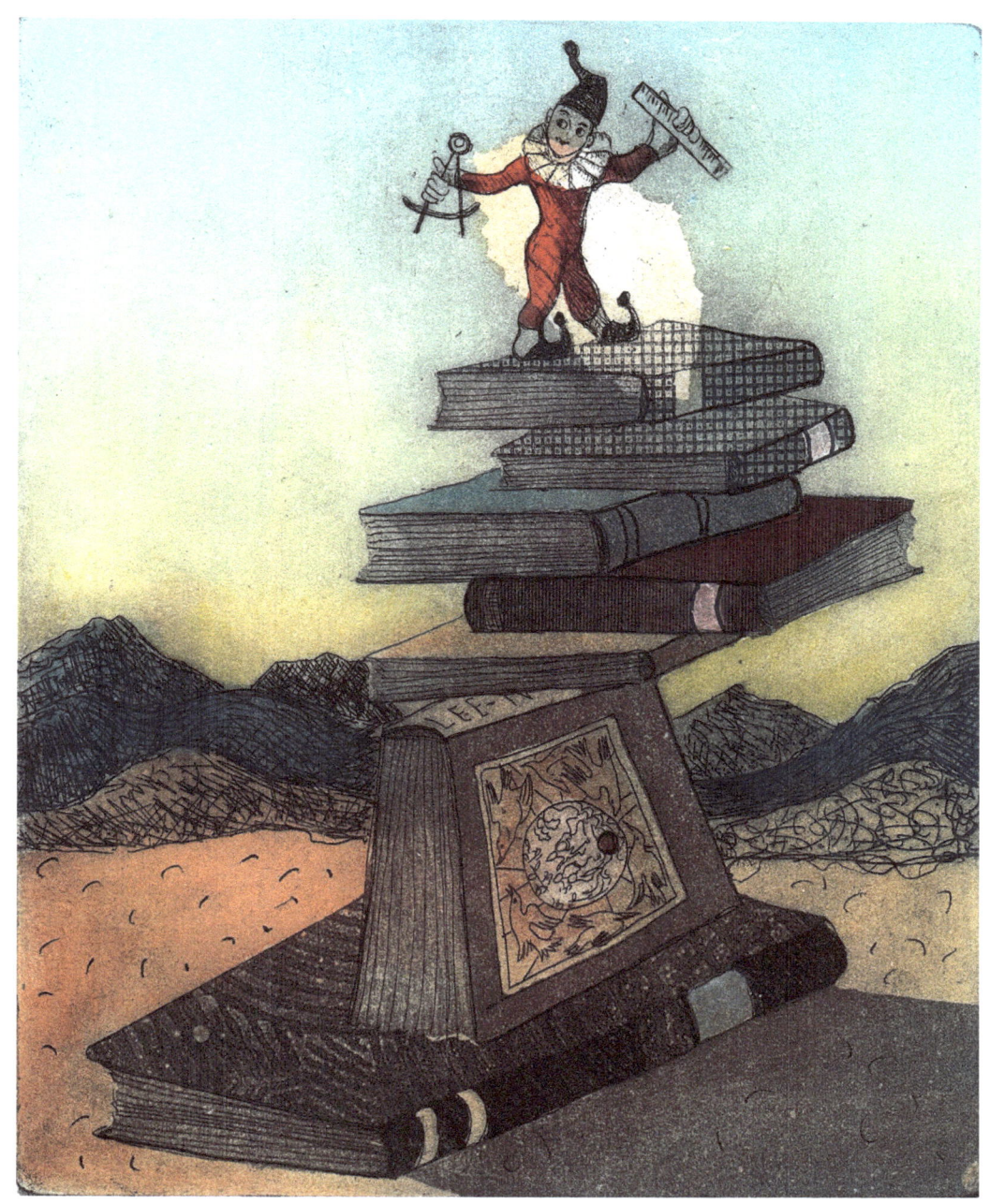

NAILED!

The Source nails me saying, "I am going to knock some sense into you. Books may give you information, but inner knowing will guide your true way in the world."

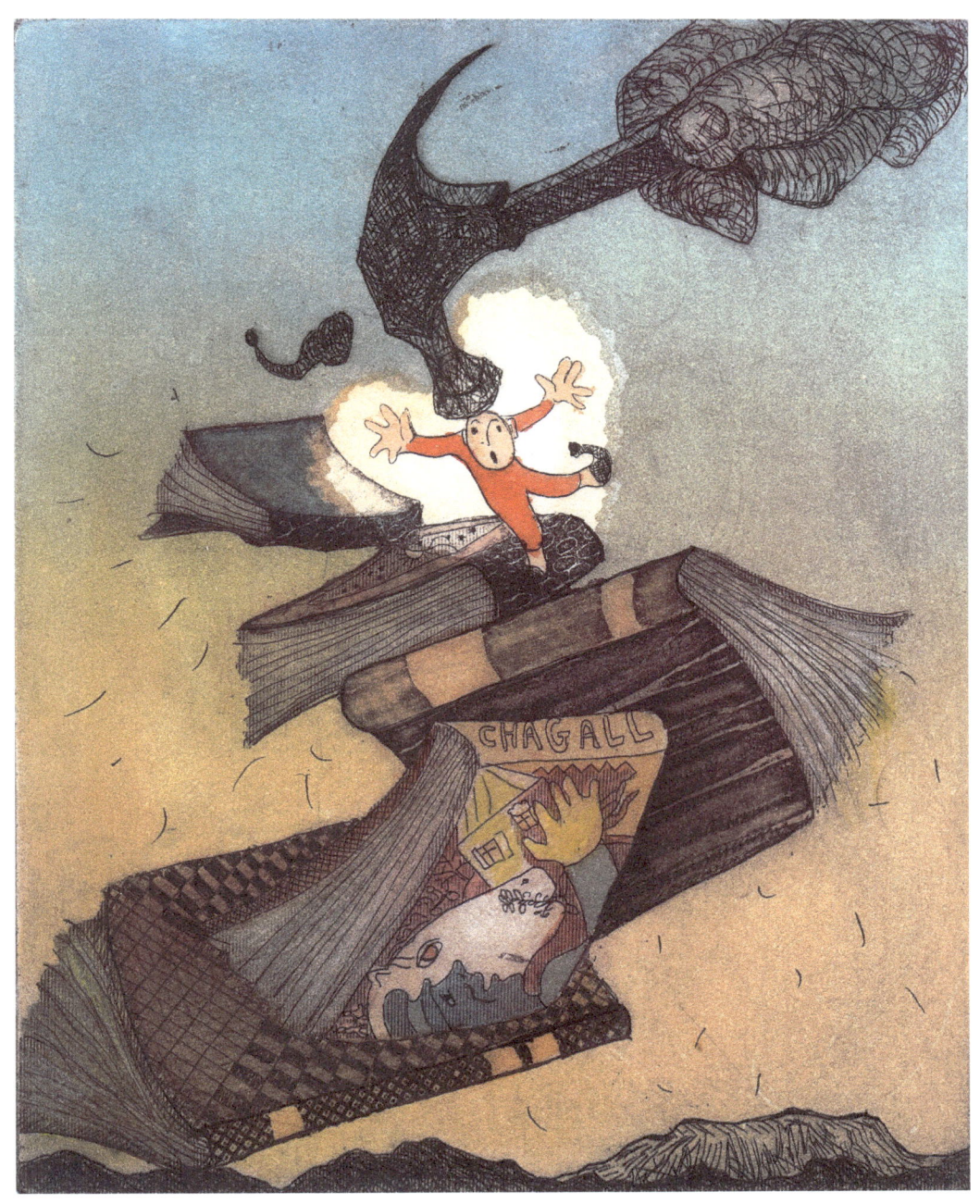

HIGH HORSE

Climbing on my High Horse I
shout, "What makes you so wise?"

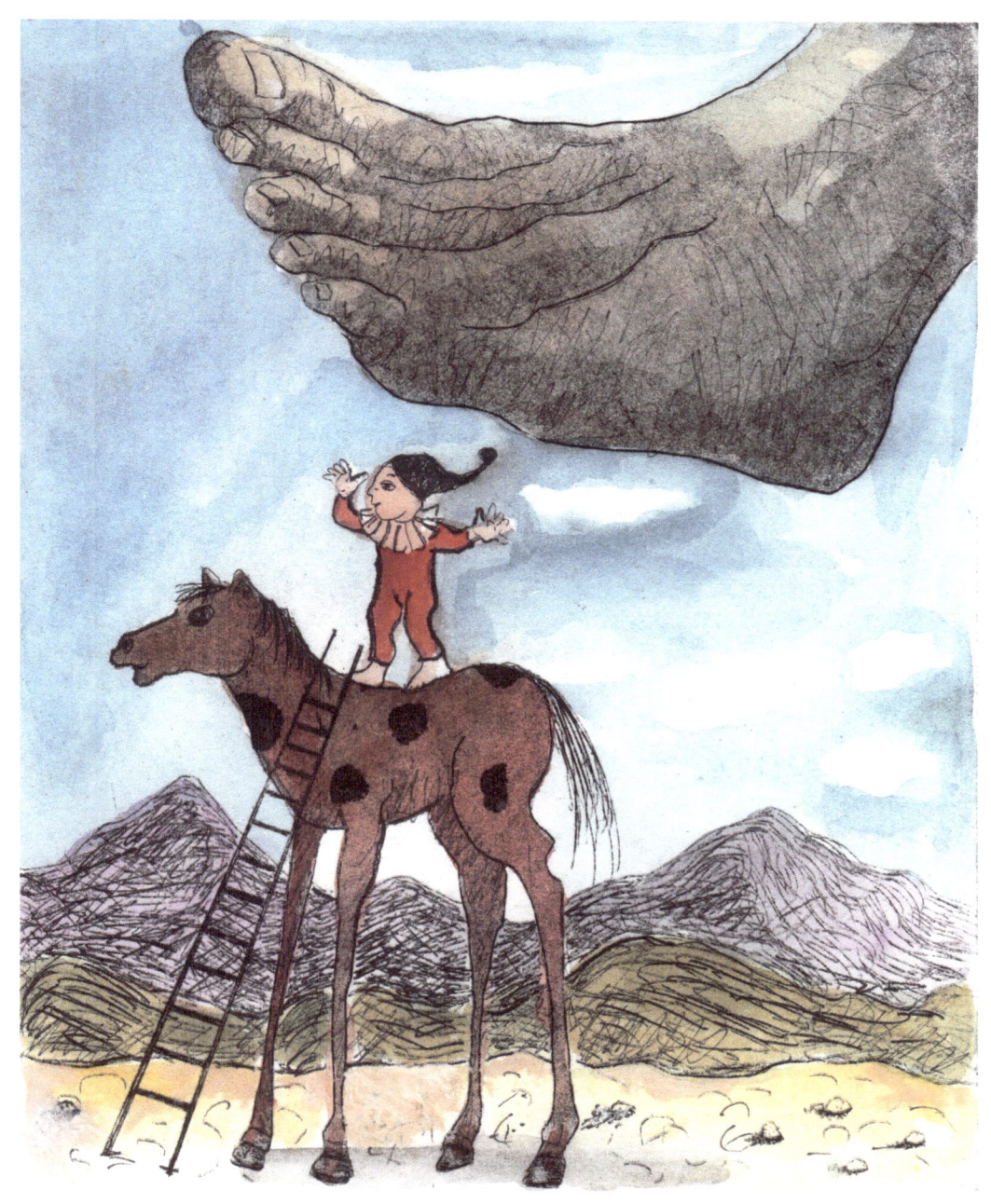

GROUND DOWN

"I am bigger than you," The
Source declares as its mighty
foot crushes me into a pancake.
My Little Self is obliterated,
scattered into a whirlwind.

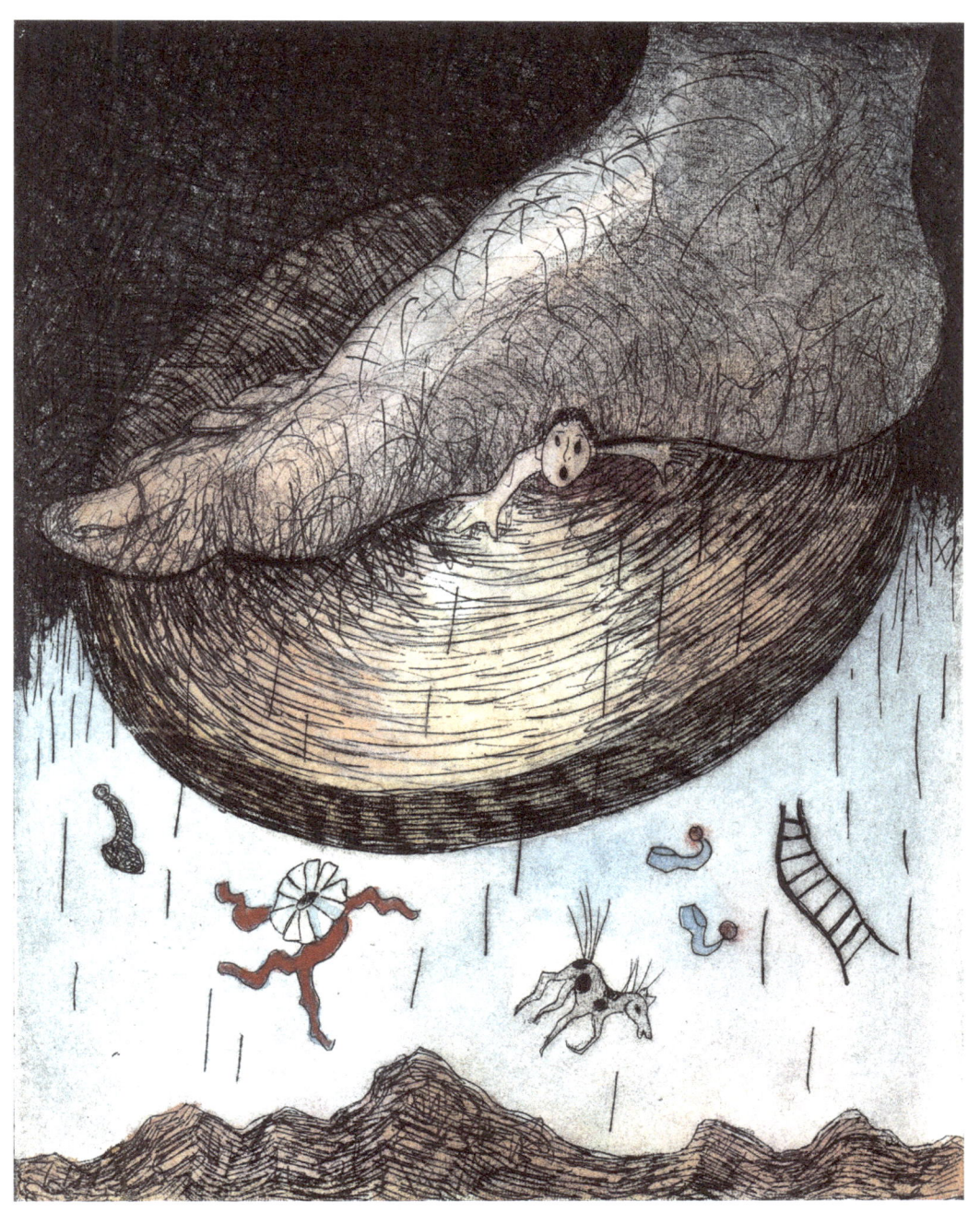

LIFTED UP!

"Enough!" I surrender, and in the moment of letting go, I am lifted up.

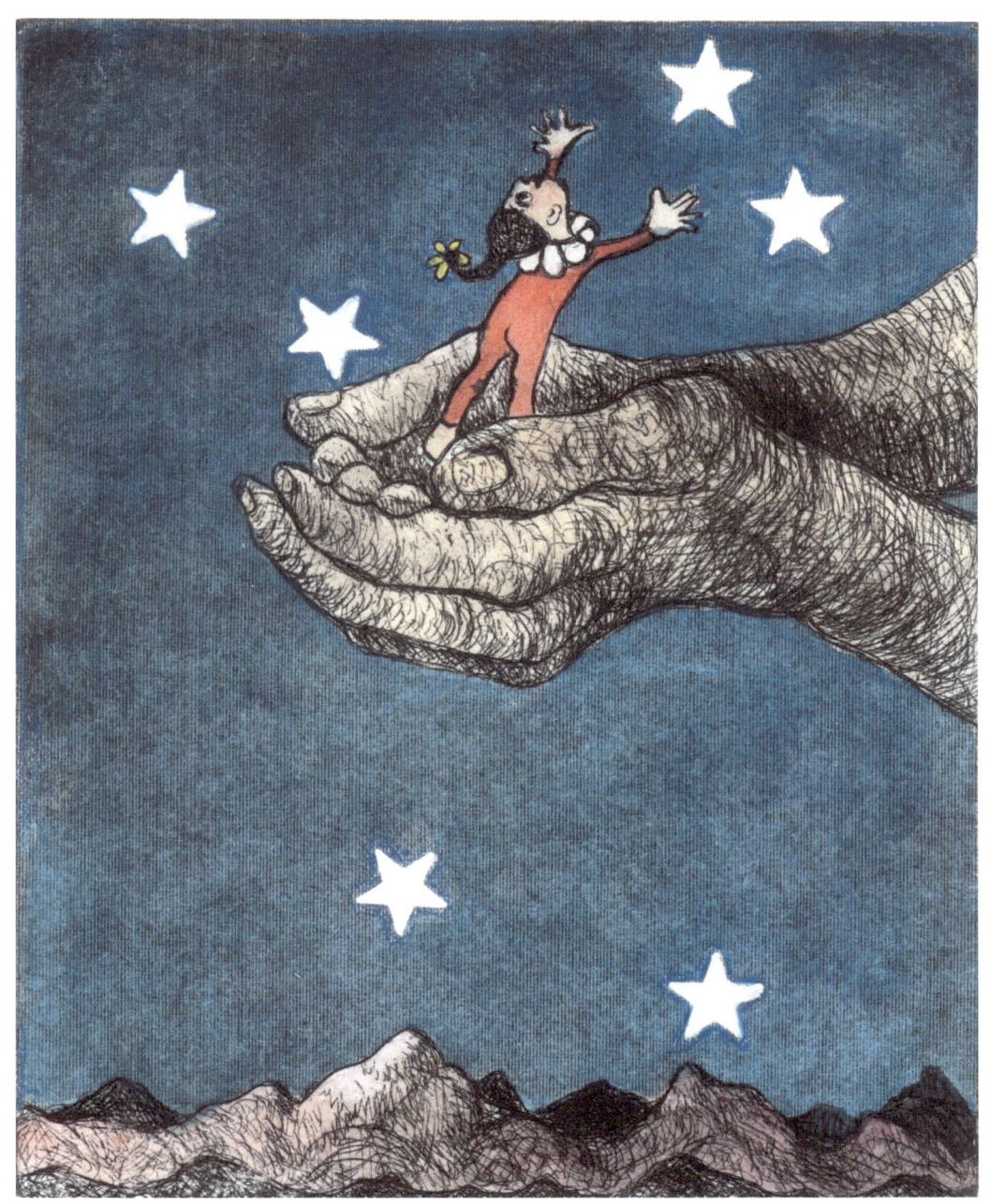

MY LUMINOUS BODY

With a swift upward movement,
my outer sheath is swept off
birthing a luminous body –
my True Self.

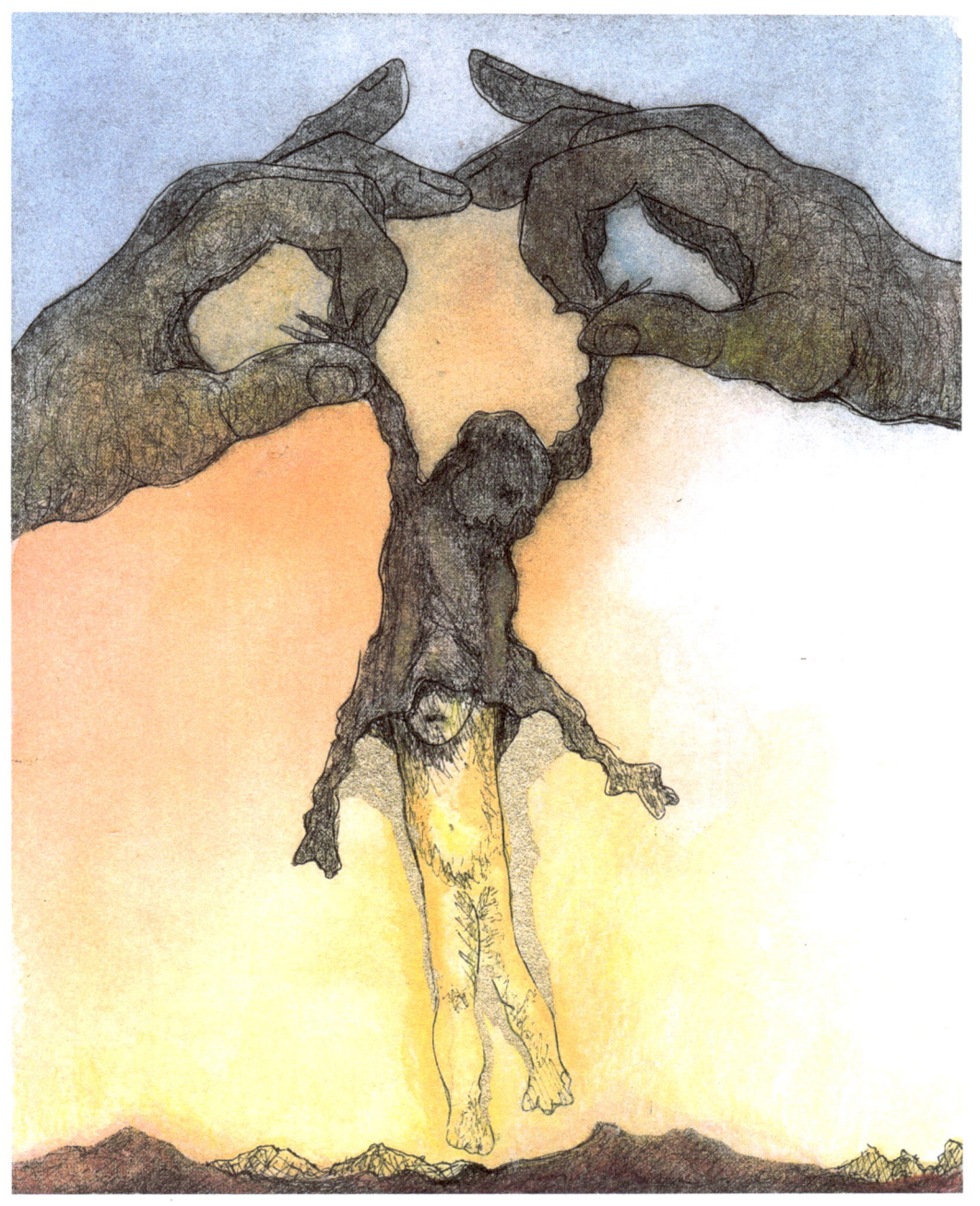

SURRENDER

I offer myself up to larger service.

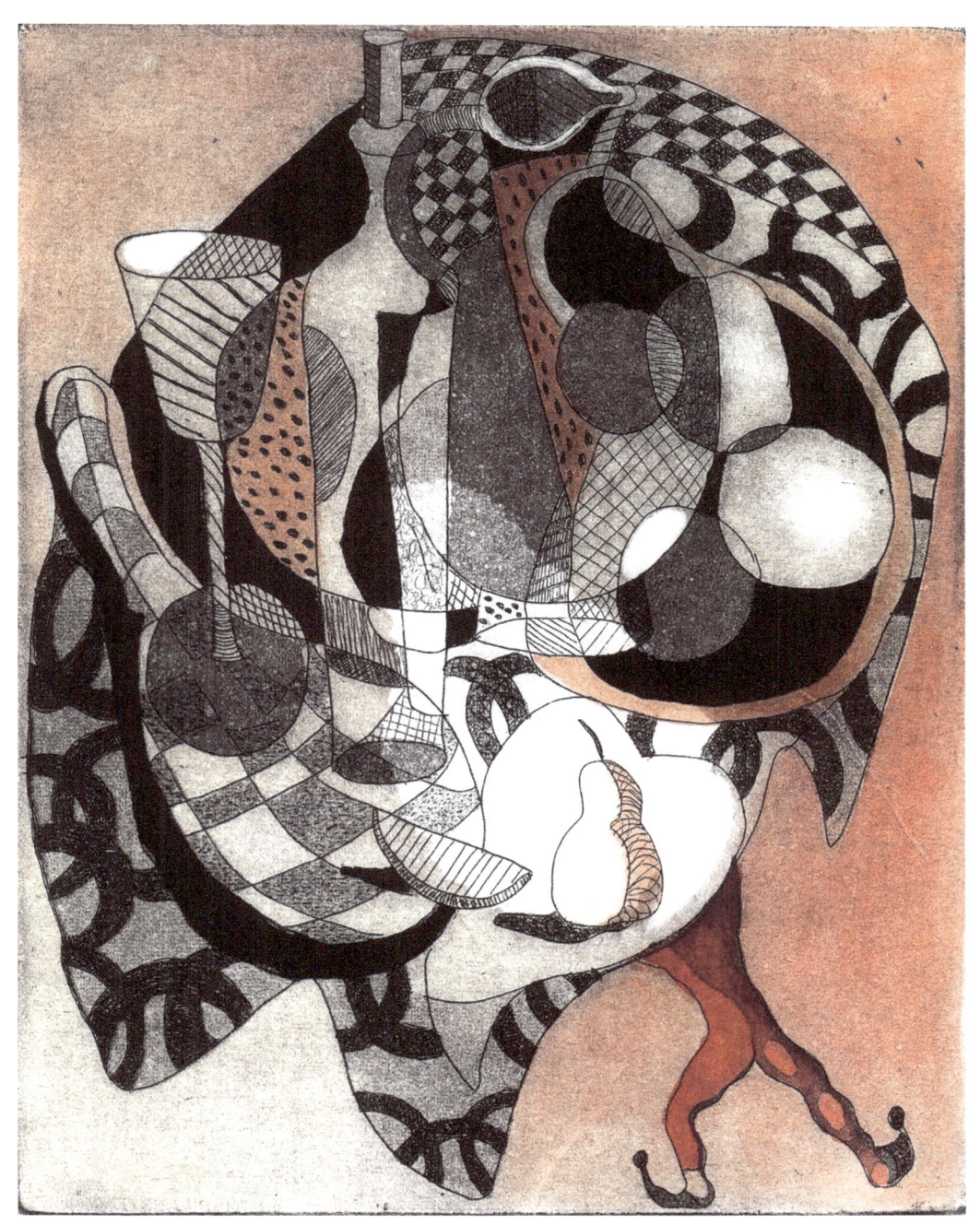

MY HEART OF GOLD

Through serving others, my heart is polished to a shining gold. Now I am ready for my teacher to appear to take me higher.

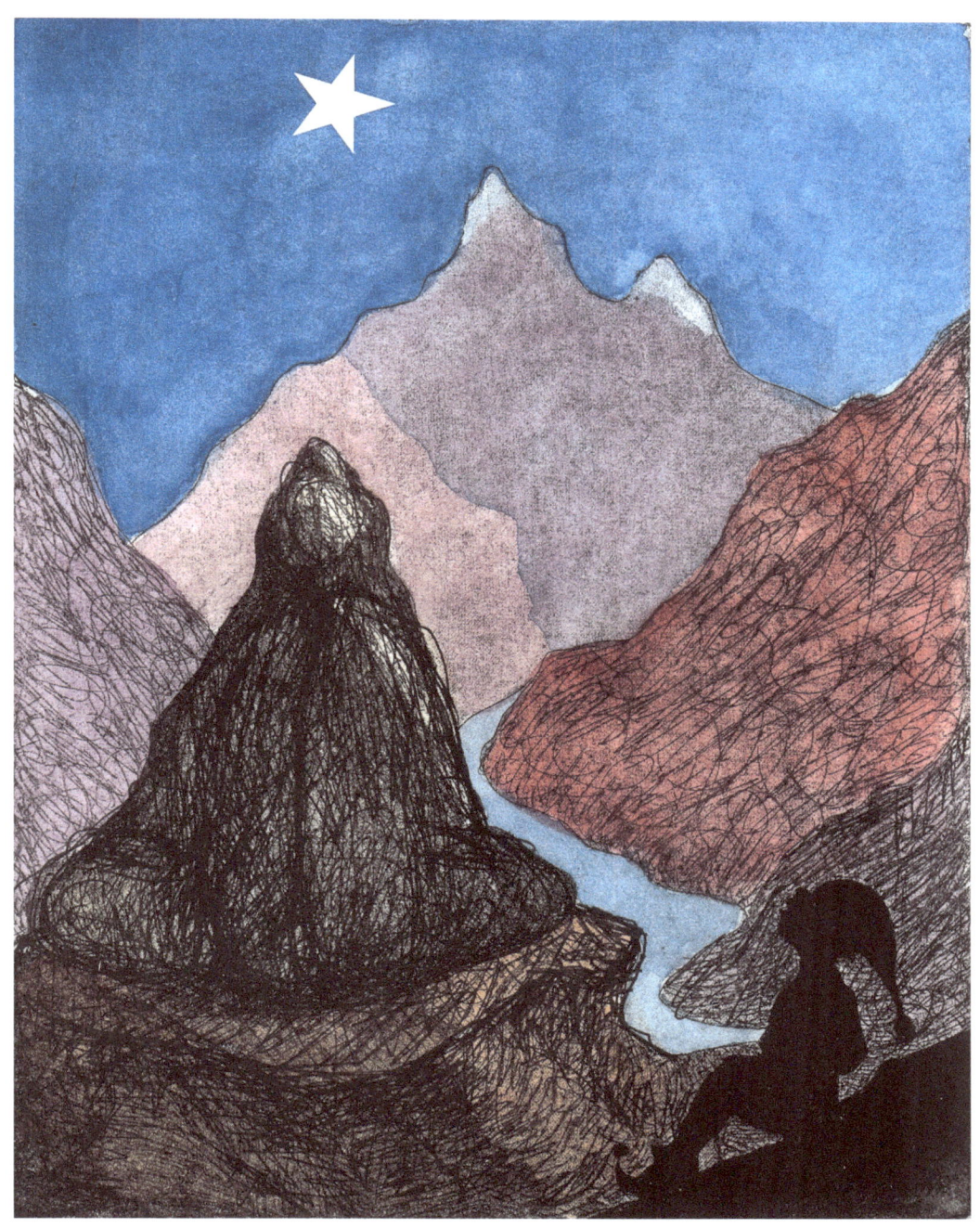

FLUTE OF ONENESS

I ride the flute of Oneness playing a lilting tune with Source. Many are called to join the dance.

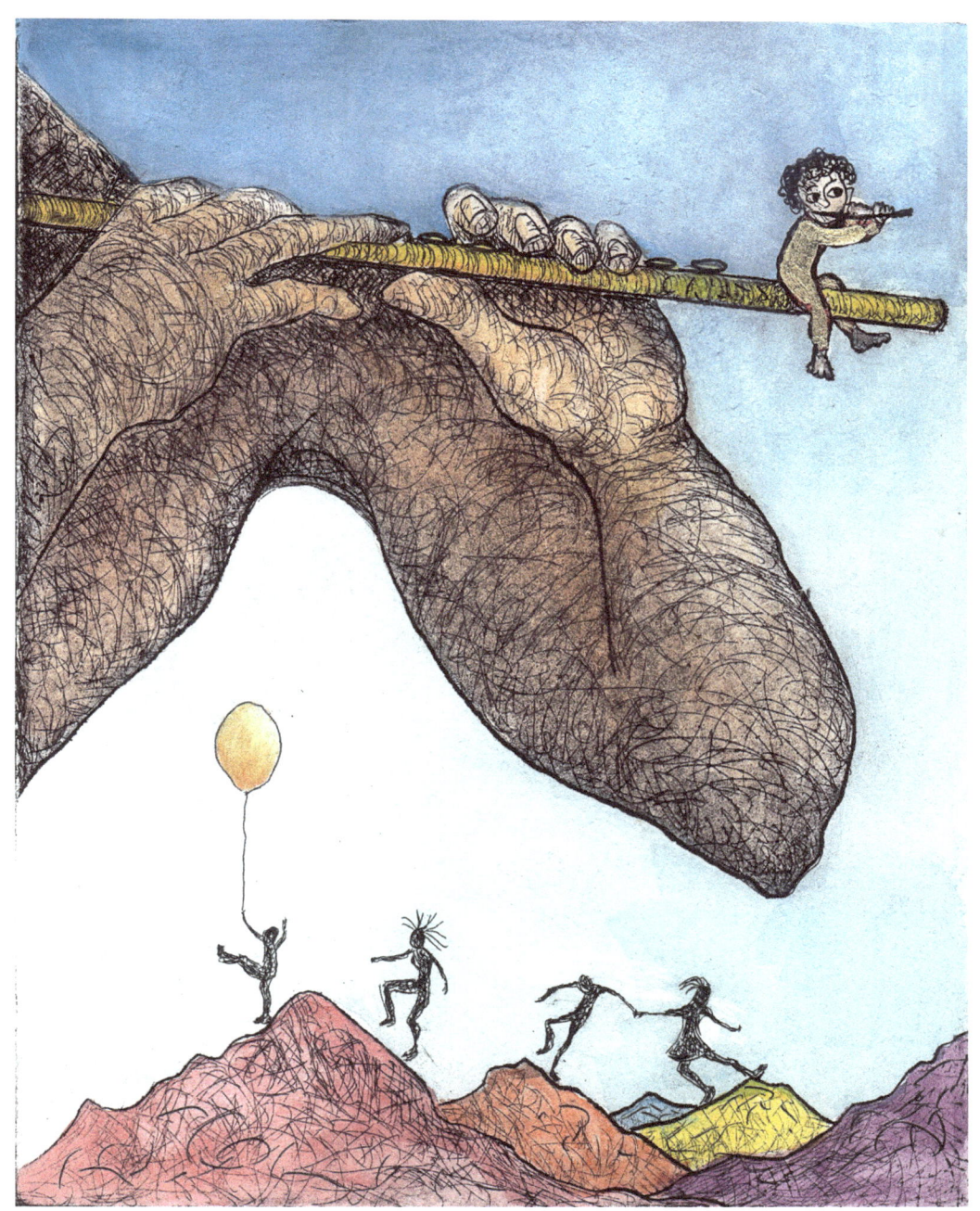

THE TREE OF LIFE BLOOMS

The tree of life bears fruit. I come full circle, joining hands with others in the eternal dance. Blossoms of delight fill our hearts.

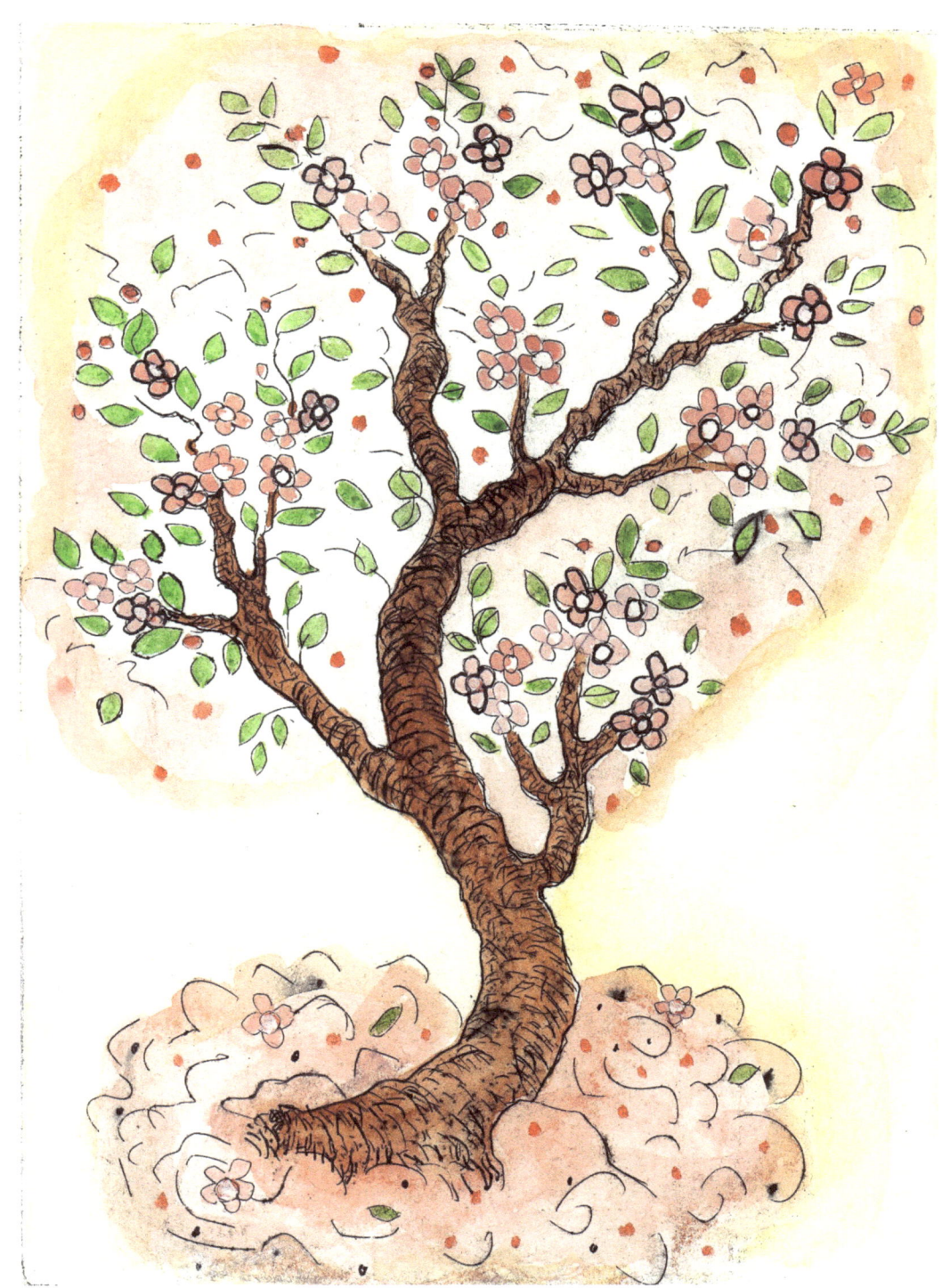

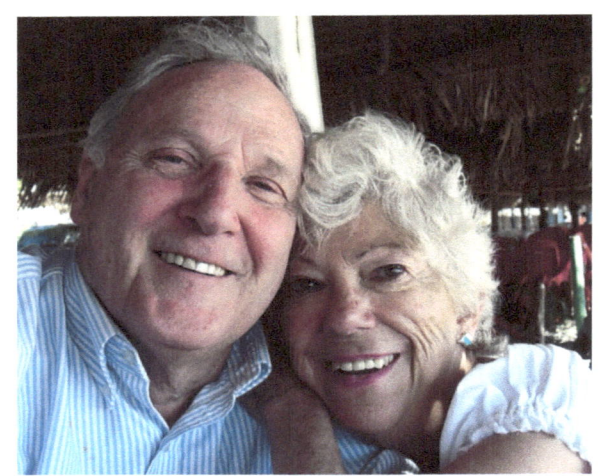

Ann Otis

lives with her partner, Bill, in New River, Arizona. She is primarily a printmaker creating etchings and monotypes. Her work has been included in numerous exhibitions and juried shows and can be found in many corporate and institutional collections including Marshall Field, Kemper Insurance, University of North Dakota, and University of Hawaii.

Recently her intaglio pieces have been emerging from her dreams and meditations. They tell a personal story, hers and maybe yours. Universal experiences are echoed in two sets of her etchings: "MY LITTLE SELF" and "JOURNEY". You will be able to interact with these images on your own terms according to your individual understanding and vision. The etchings have been put together as stories to be shared with you – and a wider audience.